A Personal Tour of
MONTICELLO

ROBERT YOUNG

LERNER PUBLICATIONS COMPANY ▪ MINNEAPOLIS

Cover: *Visitors entered the home of Thomas Jefferson by passing from the east portico, through the entrance hall, and then into the parlor.* Title page: *A painting of Monticello, dating to about 1825, shows some of the former president's younger grandchildren playing on the west lawn, while someone sketches the scene.*

The author wishes to thank Kenneth Schwarz of the Colonial Williamsburg Foundation, as well as Mindy Black, Rebecca Bowman, Ann Lucas, Zanne MacDonald, and Katherine Revell of the Thomas Jefferson Memorial Foundation, for their generous assistance; Mary Rodgers for her editorial expertise; and Sara Young and Tyler Young for their love and support.

For Paula Wilkes, an exceptional teacher

Copyright © 1999 by Robert Young

Website address: www.lernerbooks.com

LIBRARY OF CONGRESS CATALOGING-IN-PUBLICATION DATA

Young, Robert, 1951–
  A personal tour of Monticello / Robert Young
    p. cm. – (How it was)
    Includes index.
  Summary: Presents a tour of Thomas Jefferson's home in Virginia through the eyes of a slave boy, a cook, a visitor, Jefferson himself, and his granddaughter.
    ISBN 0–8225–3575–0 (lib. bdg. : alk. paper)
  1. Monticello (Va.)—Juvenile literature. 2. Jefferson, Thomas. 1743–1826—Homes and haunts—Virginia—Juvenile literature. [1. Monticello (Va.) 2. Jefferson, Thomas, 1743–1826—Homes and haunts.] I. Title   II. Series
F.332.74.Y68   1999
975.5'482—DC21   97–46662

Manufactured in the United States of America
1 2 3 4 5 6 – JR – 04 03 02 01 00 99

Contents

Oak, hickory, and chestnut trees still dominate the landscape of the small mountain on which Thomas Jefferson built his home.

Monticello is a curiosity! —Richard Rush

Introduction

Monticello was the home of Thomas Jefferson (1743–1826), one of the most famous people in U.S. history. Jefferson served as president of the United States from 1801 to 1809. During his two terms, the land area of the United States doubled in size. He wrote the Declaration of Independence and founded the University of Virginia. During his lifetime, he was also a farmer, a lawyer, a diplomat, an architect, a scientist, a husband, a father, and a grandfather.

Monticello, which means "little mountain" in Italian, sits on top of an 867-foot-high hill outside Charlottesville, a city in south central Virginia. Views from Monticello reveal woodlands, streams, and the foggy peaks of the Blue Ridge Mountains. In Jefferson's time, returning home from Washington City—about a hundred miles to the northeast—took about four days of slogging on horseback through rough, nearly roadless country.

Jefferson's father owned the land where Monticello would later be built, and young Thomas dreamed of the house he would put there. Jefferson inherited the property and, at the age of 25, began to plan his home. He drew floorplans, designed porches, and invented (and reinvented) the spaces for his own comfort and that of his family. Building Monticello took nearly 40 years. Even after all that time, it was never quite finished. For, as Jefferson is reported to have said, "Putting up and pulling down [is] one of my favorite amusements."

Jefferson centered his house on the top of the high hill. Around the house, he made four roughly circular roads, which he called roundabouts. Connected by feeder roads, the circular roads offered scenic places to walk and ride as well as pathways for goods and carriages. The closest roundabout to the house was about a half-mile in circumference (around). The three succeeding roundabouts were increasingly wider in circumference, looping around the mountain at ever-lower elevations.

Dating to the mid-1700s, Jefferson's first plan for Monticello looked very different compared to the final structure.

Stately Doric columns decorate both the east and west (shown) porticos. The former president followed some of the building ideas found in the writings of Andrea Palladio, a sixteenth-century Italian architect who admired classical styles.

When it was finished, the house had three floors. There were eleven rooms on the first floor, including Jefferson's two-room suite and his library, as well as other rooms to greet, entertain, and house visitors. On the second floor were six bedrooms. Four rooms—notably the large dome room—covered the third floor.

Jefferson designed the outside of Monticello to be made of brick. Heavy columns of the **Doric order** decorated two **porticos,** or porches. One faced east, and the other faced west. The north **piazza** (open space) led to the L-shaped north **terrace,** while on the south end he created a greenhouse that opened on to the L-shaped south terrace. After turning at a right angle, each terrace ended in a small **pavilion.** The terraces ran along the roofs of two underground service wings. Cellars and storage areas were nearest the main house. The rooms farther away, beneath the right-angle extensions, housed stables, the ice house, laundry facilities, the kitchen, and quarters for slaves.

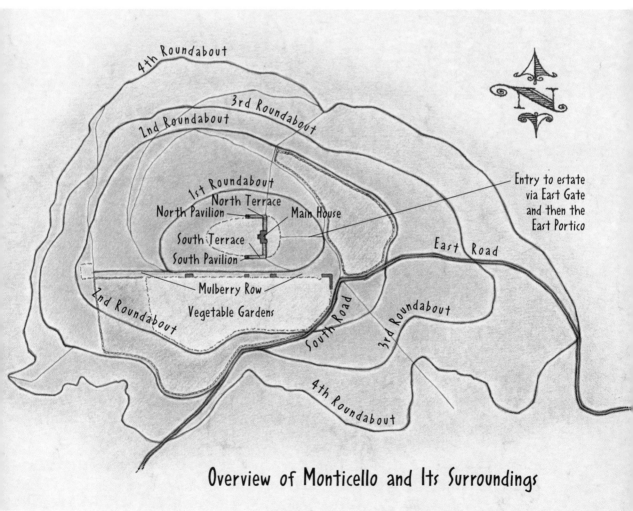

Overview of Monticello and Its Surroundings

The north terrace stretches outward from the north piazza and eventually stops at a small structure called a pavilion. The north terrace's pavilion was built nearly 40 years later than the pavilion on the south terrace.

To the south of the house, on the first roundabout, was Mulberry Row, a straight road lined with mulberry trees and buildings where some of Jefferson's many slaves lived and worked. South of Mulberry Row, Jefferson laid out the gardens and orchards that yielded enough food to feed the residents of his **plantation.** One of the largest landholders and slaveholders in Virginia, Jefferson couldn't have run his estate without the roughly 200 slaves who labored in his workshops, farmed his land, and worked in his household.

Jefferson lived at Monticello for the last 17 years of his life, and many friends and strangers made the hard journey to visit him in his mountain retreat. We'll be taking a closer look at this famous landmark through the eyes of the people who lived in, worked at, and visited Monticello. The 67-year-old former president, his only surviving daughter, and many of his grandchildren are in residence, and it's a chilly day in late May 1810.

*The space holding Jefferson's bed straddles a wall separating his
bedroom from his study. At the foot of the bed hangs his obelisk clock.*

All my wishes end where I hope my days will end, at Monticello. —Thomas Jefferson

With Thomas Jefferson

Thomas Jefferson raised his head from the pillow. He peered at the clock at the foot of his bed and could just barely see the hands in the early morning light. It was time to get up.

Jefferson had a choice to make. On which side of the bed would he get out? If he got out on one side, he would be in his bedroom. If he got out on the other side, he'd be in his cabinet (study), where he read and wrote. Jefferson's bed was built into the wall that separated these two rooms. On this spring morning, Jefferson got out on the bedroom side. He yawned and stretched his

Thomas Jefferson designed the clock that hung on a bracket at the end of his bed. It was made in Paris and replaced a similar clock that had been stolen from him. The clock was fixed between two pillars, called obelisks, made of black marble.

tall, thin body. Then he checked the thermometer and wrote down the temperature—46 degrees—in an ivory notebook.

The May air was cool, so he lit the wood that his slaves had arranged in the fireplace. As the room warmed, Jefferson soaked his bare feet in the bowl of cold water a servant had left for him, a morning routine he believed would keep him healthy. After drying his feet, he used his

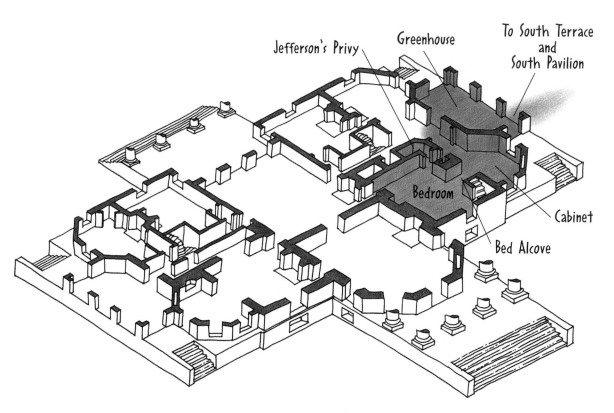

Jefferson's Map

In the greenhouse, Jefferson monitored the progress of experimental plants he'd begun from seeds.

privy—one of three bathrooms in the house. Then he went to the many-armed clothes tree in his closet, selected his clothes, and dressed.

After pulling on his boots, he headed for the south terrace to enjoy a breath of fresh air. To get to the terrace, Jefferson had to go through a door linking the bedroom and the cabinet and then exit the cabinet for the greenhouse. This glass-enclosed room faced south and held potted plants and tools. He stopped to inspect his orange tree and lightly tapped on the birdcage to say good morning to his mockingbird.

The south terrace sits atop the roof of one of the L-shaped service wings that included storage rooms and offices.

From the greenhouse, Jefferson stepped onto the terrace. From the gardens on the west lawn came the sweet scent of flowers. He hummed a tune as he walked along, admiring the bright patches of red, pink, and yellow that lined the lawn. He turned and walked to the south pavilion at the end of the terrace.

Jefferson leaned on the terrace railing and looked south toward Mulberry Row. Mule-drawn carts rattled over the dirt road as they carried charcoal, firewood, and barrels of water to the workshops. Dogs barked as they ran

The south pavilion was very special to Thomas Jefferson. In 1770 it was the first building completed at Monticello. When Jefferson married Martha Wayles Skelton in 1772, they lived in the one-room pavilion while the main house was being built. Martha died 10 years later, before Monticello was finished.

From some parts of the terrace, whose railing Jefferson designed, he could view his vegetable garden.

alongside the carts. He could hear the distant clatter of milkpans from the dairy, which lay farther down the road.

Looking beyond Mulberry Row, Jefferson could just make out the slaves hard at work in his vegetable garden. One slave slowly walked behind a plow that was turning over the reddish soil. A few slaves planted potatoes and peas. Others hoed weeds from around small corn plants.

Jefferson loved vegetables, especially English peas. His large garden provided him and his family with about 250 kinds of vegetables and herbs. Besides being a place to grow food, the garden was an experimental laboratory. Jefferson tried to raise broccoli from Italy and peppers from Mexico, and he experimented with fruit, too. His eight-acre fruit garden, which he called the fruitery, lay on the far side of the vegetable garden. Grapes and berries thrived there. So did apples, cherries, pears, plums, and 38 kinds of peaches.

Spring peas (top) *were among Jefferson's favorite vegetables. He and his neighbors competed to see which plantation owner could produce the season's first crop. The vegetable garden* (above) *sloped down from Mulberry Row.*

Jefferson walked back along the terrace and into the greenhouse. It was time for him to get to work. He headed for his cabinet and settled into the comfortable

Jefferson spent much of the morning and late afternoon working in his cabinet (study). In fact, he rarely let anyone disturb him while he was reading or writing. Among the room's ingenious pieces of equipment were a polygraph that copied letters and a revolving bookstand that could hold five volumes at a time.

Jefferson used an invention called a polygraph to copy his letters. It had two pens connected by rods made of brass and wood. Jefferson wrote his letter with one pen, while the other pen followed the exact same movements to make a copy on another sheet of paper.

chair behind his writing table. Each year Jefferson received more than a thousand letters from friends, diplomats, scholars, artists, and average citizens. He tried to respond to as many as he could. And he made copies of every letter he wrote.

As Jefferson read, a slave rolled in his breakfast on a cart. Usually he joined his family for this meal at eight o'clock, but on this day he wanted to enjoy the tasty corn bread, cold ham, and coffee while he worked. Later in the day, about one o'clock, he'd order his horse brought around so he could go for his daily ride. He would check on the activity in the shops, talk with the overseers, and survey the work on the farms and in the gardens. It was going to be another busy day for Thomas Jefferson.

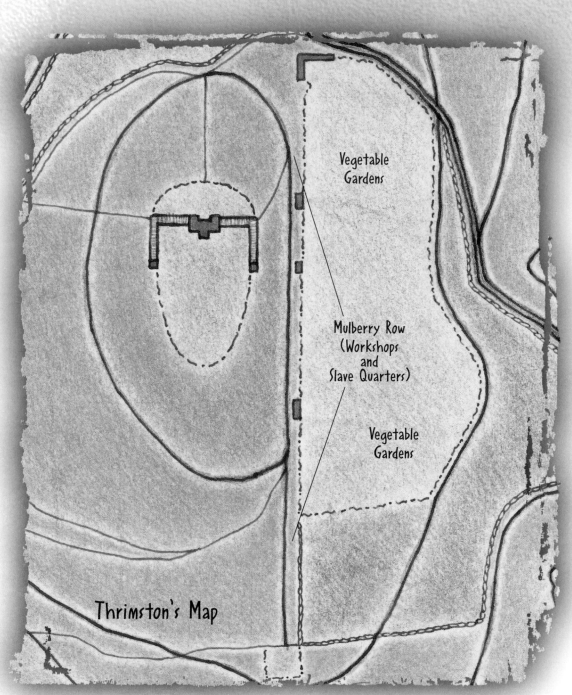

Vegetable
Gardens

Mulberry Row
(Workshops
and
Slave Quarters)

Vegetable
Gardens

Thrimston's Map

*Shops and dwellings lined Mulberry Row, the long straight section of
one of Monticello's four circular roads, called roundabouts.*

Isaac . . . [carried] on the nail business at
Monticello seven years. —Isaac Jefferson

With Thrimston

Ten-year-old Thrimston stood in the nail shop. Sweat dripped down his face and dropped to the dirt floor. Working near a fire made him hot. Too hot. But Thrimston had no choice. He was one of Thomas Jefferson's slaves at Monticello. Thrimston's job was to make nails. He worked from sunrise to sunset, six days a week.

Thrimston was out of nailrod. He needed to go to the storehouse to get more. After telling Grady,

Nailrod, the metal used to manufacture nails, was made of thin strips of iron. Monticello's nailrod came from Philadelphia, Pennsylvania—several hundred miles away. Large and small ships carried the material upriver to Richmond, Virginia, and then to the small town of Milton. Wagons brought the nailrod overland from Milton to Monticello. Because a new order of nailrod might take several months to arrive, Jefferson bought a ton at a time.

Most of Jefferson's slaves lived in log cabins. Although he treated his slaves better than most slaveholders, Jefferson still chose to use slave labor instead of paid labor on his estate.

Not long ago, Thrimston had spent his days at home. There had been lots of jobs—letting out the chickens in the morning, working in the garden, and helping watch the younger children. He also had had time to play with the other slave children and even with Mr. Jefferson's grandchildren at the main house. But at the age of 10, Thrimston had been put to work in the nail shop. And he knew he had to get back there fast. The overseer might notice he'd been gone for a while, and Thrimston would be in trouble. Luckily Grady didn't whip the boys as the last overseer had.

Thrimston took some more hoe cake and said good-bye to his mother. He ran back to the storehouse, grabbed some nailrod, and carried it into the nail shop. Grady weighed the nailrod, writing the amount in a small book. At the end of the day, he'd weigh the nails each boy had made. He'd then compare the amount to the quantity of nailrod in the notebook to find out how much nailrod each boy had wasted. Mr. Jefferson wanted to know who was his most efficient nail maker. Thrimston wanted to be the best, because the overseer often gave extra food, sometimes money, or even clothes to the best workers.

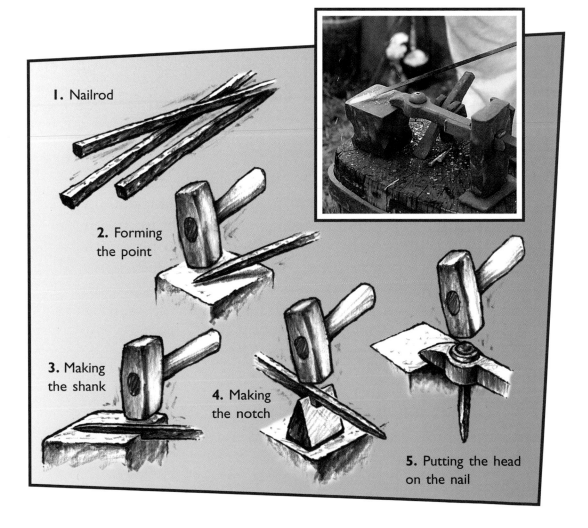

1. Nailrod

2. Forming the point

3. Making the shank

4. Making the notch

5. Putting the head on the nail

Thrimston looked around. The other boys were hard at work. There were nine of them, laboring around two fires. The overseer stood nearby, inspecting the finished nails. Thrimston picked up his hammer, tongs, and other tools. To stoke the fire, he squeezed the bellows, a device that forced air into the fire and made the coals glow bright red. Then he grabbed a three-foot-long piece of nailrod and placed one end into the hot coals. Within two minutes, the end turned red, orange, yellow, then white. The smell of coal and burning metal filled his nostrils.

Thrimston lifted the rod and laid it flat on his anvil. Clang! He struck the rod with his hammer, flattening the end. Clang! Then he turned the rod and struck it again, making sure the point at the end formed evenly. Thrimston lifted the rod to the edge of the anvil and hammered, making a deep crease that would be the shoulder (shank) of the nail.

Thrimston next laid the rod on a sharp tool called a hardie that looked like an upended chisel. He pounded the rod with his hammer until a notch was cut in the metal above the spot where he'd made the shoulder crease. Then he stuck the pointed end of the nail into the header, a small hole on top of the anvil. He bent back the rod, which snapped off at the notch. Then he pounded down on the rounded metal still sticking out above the hole, making a head for the nail. The nail was finished. With small tongs, Thrimston lifted the still-red-hot nail from the header and dropped it on the dirt floor to cool.

Thrimston made another nail. And another. And another. Soon his hammer was the only one heard in the shop. Thrimston looked around him. Outside he could see

Much of what is known about slave life at Monticello comes from the remembrances of Isaac Jefferson, who was born into slavery on Jefferson's estate in 1775. He worked in and later managed the plantation's nailery, where he recalled, "Mr. Jefferson...gave the boys...a pound of meat a week, a dozen herrings, a quart of molasses and peck of meal." In the 1820s, Isaac Jefferson helped take care of the aging former president. In the late 1840s, the one-time slave was interviewed at length by Charles Campbell.

the sun was high in the sky. It was about midday, and the overseer had left. Two of the boys were wrestling on the floor. The others were sitting on boxes along the wall.

Thrimston put down his hammer and sat with the other boys. A few were laughing and joking. But one was serious. He was talking about running away. Running away was risky. What if he got caught? He could be brought back and whipped. He might even get sold to another slaveholder. One of the boys said Mr. Jefferson was a lot better than most. What would it be like to be free, Thrimston wondered.

An idyllic drawing shows slaves welcoming Thomas Jefferson home to Monticello.

At this time in the United States, slaves were considered property and had few legal rights. Laws even made it legal to kill a runaway slave. One of the largest slaveholders in Virginia, Jefferson kept his slaves well fed and clothed. He took care of their medical needs and tried hard to keep slave families together. During his lifetime, Jefferson freed two slaves and allowed two more to escape. In his will, he set five more free.

Why didn't he free more? At his death, Jefferson was heavily in debt. In fact, Monticello had never been out of debt. Without the unpaid labor of slaves, Monticello couldn't operate, and Jefferson couldn't live the way he wanted. Jefferson also believed, as did many landholders of his time, that most slaves were unskilled and would not be able to support themselves. All seven of the slaves Jefferson freed had learned trades, which he thought would enable them to make a living.

When Grady returned, he shouted at the boys to get back to work. They scrambled to their feet and went back to their fires. As Thrimston began making a new nail, the overseer told him to get more charcoal to feed the fire. Thrimston grabbed two buckets and ran out the door, happy to get another break from his hot and boring job.

As he passed the blacksmith's shop, he could smell the hot metal and the burning charcoal. Slaves were shoeing horses, fixing plows, and making gun parts. Farther down Mulberry Row, Thrimston passed the joinery, where slaves put together pieces of wood to make tables, chairs, and carriage parts. They also created woodwork for the main house.

Not far from the joinery was the carpenter's shop. The shop was quiet. Some of the carpenters were working on the roof of the main house. The others were out cutting trees for fences, shingles, or firewood. Thrimston passed the sawpit where sawyers cut logs into lumber. He wondered if he would be a sawyer someday. Or would he be a field worker like his father and brother? He might be a house servant or learn a trade.

Thrimston thought a house servant had the best life for a slave. They got better clothes and better food, and they had more time to themselves. Learning a trade wouldn't be bad either. He could see himself as a blacksmith or a cabinetmaker or even a shoemaker.

Thrimston had no choice in what he would become. In four to six years, Mr. Jefferson would decide what trade Thrimston would learn. In the meantime, though, Thrimston could show Mr. Jefferson what a good worker he was. He quickly filled his buckets with charcoal and lugged them back to the nail shop.

The ex-president encouraged his family and visitors to borrow books from his library, which he organized by subject for easy reference.

My grandfather's manners to us, his grandchildren, were delightful.... He talked with us freely, affectionately... —Ellen Randolph Coolidge

With Cornelia Jefferson Randolph

Cornelia Jefferson Randolph, nearly 11 years old, tugged on the brass chain that held the alabaster lamp. As she pulled, the beautiful white lamp slowly rose toward the ceiling of the library. The lamp was clean, thanks to Cornelia and her sisters. Her Grandpapa would be happy about that.

After they'd finished their breakfast, all the children had chores to do. Cornelia didn't like doing housework, but she enjoyed cleaning the alabaster lamp. The task gave her a chance to be in the library, where Grandpapa did much of his reading and studying. Usually the door was locked, and no one was allowed in without being invited.

Cornelia slid onto the tall chair that stood in one corner of the room. She pressed her cheek against the cool red leather and looked around. Thousands of books filled the shelves. She could see the gold lettering on the red, brown, and black spines and could smell their leather bindings. Cornelia wondered if she could read this many books in her whole life.

Her methodical Grandpapa had carefully organized his library. He kept science and history volumes in one area, while law and math titles were in another. Books about

(Left) *The library's shelves were actually the packing crates Jefferson had used to ship his books.* (Below) *The alabaster lamp—a gift to Jefferson from his grandson Thomas Jefferson Randolph—was on a pulley system that enabled it to be lit and cleaned easily.*

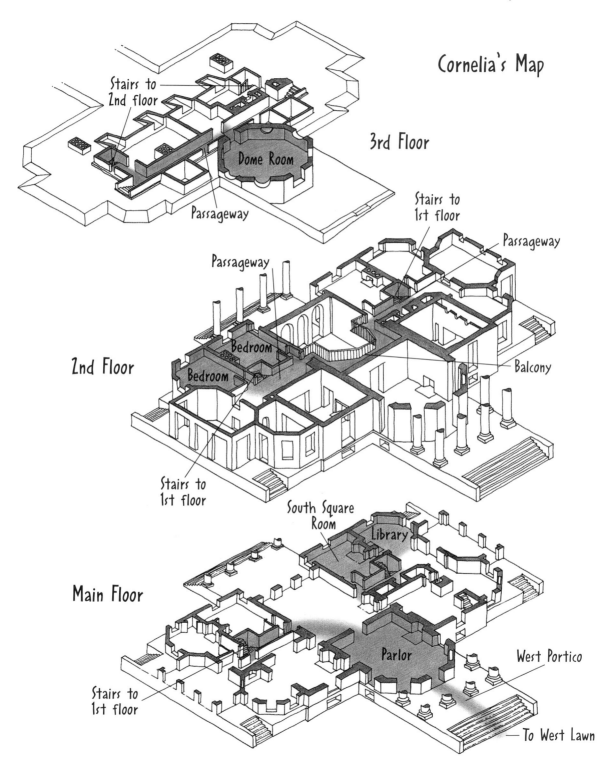

Cornelia's Map

3rd Floor

Stairs to
2nd floor

Dome Room

Passageway

Stairs to
1st floor

Passageway

2nd Floor

Passageway

Bedroom

Bedroom

Balcony

Stairs to
1st floor

Main Floor

South Square
Room

Library

Parlor

West Portico

Stairs to
1st floor

To West Lawn

the arts were together, too. He even had a catalog to help him keep track of all his holdings.

Soon her thoughts were interrupted by the voice of her mother calling Cornelia to her studies. Cornelia and her sisters didn't have to travel to school in Richmond like her older brother did. They had only to walk into the next room, the family sitting room. The room was small, but there was enough space for each child to work.

Cornelia picked up her books from the shelf by the window and sat at the desk tucked into the corner. She didn't wait for her mother to tell her what her lessons were for the day. She began on her own. Cornelia loved to

Cornelia lived at Monticello with six of her eight brothers and sisters. Cornelia's mother was Martha Jefferson Randolph *(pictured left)*, Jefferson's only surviving child, whom he called Patsy. The little girl's father was Thomas Mann Randolph, who ran a nearby farm.

Cornelia's father could not support his large family, and the widowed Jefferson needed a hostess for Monticello. So Martha—along with Ellen, Cornelia, Virginia, Mary, James, Benjamin, and Meriwether—took up residence at Monticello. (The eldest child, Anne, was married, and the eldest son, Thomas Jefferson Randolph, was away at school. In 1814 and 1818, Martha had two more children, who would also live at Monticello.)

Positioned next to the library, the family sitting room was also known as the south square room because of its location and shape. On the floor is the children's game goose and feathers. Above the mantle is a portrait of Jefferson's daughter Martha.

learn. She studied geography, history, and French. She worked on math problems and memorized poems. Cornelia practiced writing with a quill pen and ink. To improve her drawing, she used a special device called a camera obscura that Grandpapa had bought.

Every day, after breakfast and chores, Cornelia and her sisters studied. Cornelia also learned to paint with watercolors and to play the harpsichord. Her mother taught her to sew, and her grandfather showed her how to garden. Drawing was one of her favorite activities.

At about two o'clock, studies were over for the day. Cornelia climbed the steep stairs to the second floor, her

The camera obscura had a lens and a mirror that reflected the image of an object onto a viewing plate. By putting paper over the viewing plate, the image could be traced. Jefferson thought that this device would help his grandchildren improve their ability to draw.

long dress brushing against the narrow stairway. At the top of the stairs, she walked along the balcony and looked down into the entrance hall. Cornelia was surprised to see the room empty. Usually a visitor was waiting to meet Grandpapa. It seemed as if there was always someone visiting Monticello.

Cornelia turned the corner into her bedroom. The room was one of six on the second floor. Like most of the others, it had a single square window on the wall just above the floor. It might seem a strange place for a window, but Cornelia knew the reason it was there. Grandpapa had designed the house to look as if it had only one story, like French townhouses. To do this, he tricked the eye. From the outside, the second-floor windows looked like they were part of the first-floor windows. What a clever man he was!

Cornelia had finished her studies, but she still wanted to read. Thump! Thump! Bang! But loud noises distracted her. Someone was up on the third floor. She walked out to the hall and snuck up the stairs to the next floor. Cornelia was right. Four of her brothers and sisters were playing hide and seek in the dome room. Although the eight round windows and the skylight allowed light to fill the room, it was being used for storage so there were lots of things to hide behind. Cornelia joined in the fun, helping her little brothers, James and Benjamin, find good

Jefferson based some of Monticello's windows on a style he'd admired in France. On the first floor, these windows were placed high. On the second floor, they rose just above the floor. From the outside, the house appeared to have only one floor lit by one set of windows, when actually the windows illuminated two floors.

The dome room on the third floor had its own set of windows—eight circular openings and an overhead skylight.

hiding spots. Later they all went down to the second floor to the bedroom of her younger sister Mary. They played another of their favorites, a board game called goose and feathers.

As they were putting away the game, Virginia, another of Cornelia's younger sisters, looked out the square window. A slave was walking Grandpapa's horse. He must be back from his ride! Virginia ran for the door, followed by Cornelia and the other grandchildren.

Thump! And thump again! They rushed out of the bedroom, down the steep staircase, and through the parlor.

After bursting through the door of the west portico, they felt the warmth of the late afternoon sun.

Grandpapa was happy to see them, and he had a kind word for each child. He led the children along the winding walkway that surrounded the west lawn, pointing out the colorful lilies and larkspur that lined the path. Cornelia was proud of the flower gardens, which she had helped plant earlier in the spring.

Burwell, the butler, soon came from the house. He told Grandpapa there was a guest waiting in the entrance hall. The children begged him to stay longer, but they knew he had to go. Cornelia watched as Grandpapa walked toward the house. She loved the time he spent with them. If only it could be more!

Jefferson carefully planned the flower beds that surrounded the west lawn. Visitors and family members could meander along the pathway, enjoying the sights and smells of lilies, larkspur, roses, and sweet peas.

A large room with good sunlight, the main kitchen at Monticello had many conveniences and innovations.

With Edith Fossett

Edith Fossett, often called Edy, stretched as she stood in Monticello's kitchen, which was located under the southeast corner of the south terrace. It was a big room, larger than her own quarters, and had been built far from the main rooms of the house. The kitchen and its windows faced south, allowing bright sunlight to filter in, even in the winter. The walls were plaster, and the floor was brick. Drying herbs hung from the timbers that supported the ceiling.

Monticello's kitchen was not close to the main part of the house. There were two chief reasons—to keep away dangerous fires and offensive odors. Because cooks prepared food over open fireplaces, a chance always existed for an accident to happen. Separating the kitchen from the dining room also kept away the bad smells of food that had spoiled from lack of refrigeration.

Edith and Fanny, both slaves, cooked for Mr. Jefferson. Their job was to make sure he and his family and guests were properly fed. Honoré Julien, the French chef who'd been with Mr. Jefferson when he was president, had trained Edith and Fanny while they were all at the President's House in Washington. Julien's meals had been legendary.

Edith walked to the stew stove under the window. It was like the one she'd used in Washington. It was waist high and had eight stew-holes, or burners, on the top where food in pots could be heated. Below each stew-hole was a small section to burn charcoal. By varying the amount of coal, foods could be cooked at the same time but at different temperatures.

Mr. Jefferson had designed a fine kitchen. In addition to the stove with the stew-holes, there was an open hearth with a spit and jack (a device for turning the spit) and two bake ovens. The cooks had nearly everything they could want— tin-lined copper pots, sauce and sauté pans, ice-cream molds, waffle irons, and even a macaroni maker! Mr. Jefferson had bought some of these things in France when he'd lived there.

Jefferson went to France in 1784 and began to serve a four-year term as the U.S. minister to the French royal court in 1785. During this period, he bought many things for Monticello, including books, paintings, furniture, linens, china, flatware, and kitchen equipment. Expertly packed in 86 crates, his purchases, including 15 cases of books, arrived in 1790.

Edith rubbed her eyes. Although Mr. Jefferson had provided the latest utensils, the kitchen was still not an easy place to work. The vapors were strong, the fires were

Edith's Map

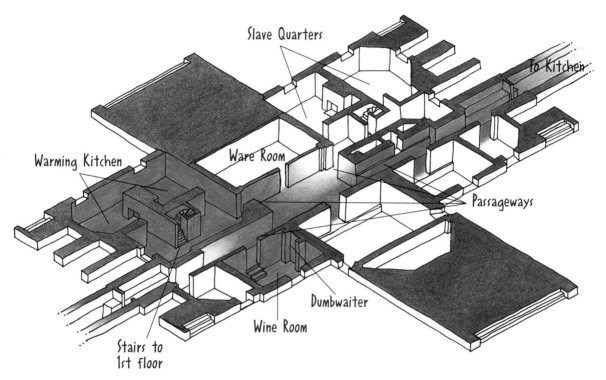

Slave Quarters

To Kitchen

Warming Kitchen

Ware Room

Passageways

Dumbwaiter

Wine Room

Stairs to
1st floor

hot, and the constant smoke made her eyes burn. Straightening her back, she took the lid off one of the pots on the stove and stirred the bubbling contents. Edith sniffed. The applesauce smelled good and would go well with the goose that was roasting on the hearth.

It was late in the afternoon, nearly time for dinner. The kitchen became a flurry of activity. Fanny garnished the pie made of oysters and sweetbreads (calves' glands). Waiters prepared the food platters they'd carry along the covered underground passageway that ran the length and width of the house. Edith's children helped grind the mocha coffee beans—Mr. Jefferson's favorite—and earlier had shelled peas from the garden.

Thirteen-year-old Ellen Wayles Randolph paced the floor of the kitchen. As they got older, Mr. Jefferson's granddaughters took turns being in charge of the kitchen at Monticello. Ellen carried the keys to the rooms where the food and wine were kept. After consulting with her mother, Ellen had chosen the menu and was ready to set aside the wines.

She greeted Edith, asked about the dinner preparations, and told Edith to check on the warming kitchen. Turning the stove over to Fanny, Edith grabbed the metal ice-cream molds to take with her. There would be ice cream for dinner, but it would be made near the dining room.

Edith walked along the passageway under the house. It was dark, but the air was cool and felt good after being in the hot, smoky kitchen. At the wine room, Ellen was opening the thick wooden door with her key. Edith

A covered, all-weather passageway linked the service areas of the house, including the kitchen, the laundry, the stables, and the smoke room.

The wine cellar kept Jefferson's store of vintages at the proper temperature. The dumbwaiter— used for delivering freshly decanted bottles—was hidden in the mantelpiece of the dining room, which was located above the cellar.

stepped in and watched as Ellen picked the wines for dinner. Later Burwell would decant (pour out) her choices and load them on a dumbwaiter, a device that carried the wine up to the dining room by way of a rope pulley system.

After Ellen locked the wine room, she walked with Edith along the passageway. They passed another locked room—the ware room—that had most of the food stored in it. Midway along the passageway, they reached the small warming kitchen near the stairs that led up to the dining room.

Edith set down the ice-cream molds and checked to see that all was ready. In the warming room, the servants would put the finishing touches on the meals before taking them upstairs. As Ellen climbed the stairs to the dining room, Edith began walking quickly back to the kitchen. It was almost dinnertime. And there was so much left to do.

The entrance hall—with its paintings, busts of famous people, and Native American artifacts—gave Monticello a museumlike quality.

Almost every day, for at least eight months of the year, brought its contingent of guests.

—Ellen Randolph Coolidge

With a Visitor

The visitor stood in the middle of the entrance hall. It was late afternoon, and he was exhausted from the long and bumpy carriage ride up the oak-and-hickory-studded mountain. The circular roads leading to Monticello had given the visitor a chance to anticipate his first view of the house through the east gate.

Although tired, the visitor was excited, too. Soon he would be paying his respects to Mr. Thomas Jefferson, a man he admired very much. The visitor dug his hand into his coat pocket to check for his letter of introduction. Yes, it was still there.

The visitor looked around the hall as he waited for his host. The ceiling was high, and the room was light and airy. There were many chairs but not much other furniture. What a perfect spot to begin a visit to Monticello! The visitor had heard that the entrance hall told a lot about the

The entrance hall's clock hangs on the wall over the door and has two faces. The inside one shows the hour, minute, and second. The other face, indicating only the hour, can be seen from the outside on the portico.

Jefferson designed the clock to be run by metal weights. As the clock ran, the weights moved down the wall and showed the days of the week as they passed by markers. Every Sunday the clock had to be wound with a cranklike key.

man who designed and lived in this grand home in the Blue Ridge Mountains.

The room held much to admire. Moose and elk antlers hung on the wall. There were paintings and Native American artifacts. The visitor counted 10 different maps. Flanking the door were busts of famous thinkers, like Voltaire and Turgot. Sculpted images of Alexander Hamilton, Mr. Jefferson's political opponent, and of Mr. Jefferson himself stood in the corners. Near them were interesting stone-carved faces. It was hard to take it all in—bones, fossils, shells, minerals, and crystals, too.

When the visitor heard footsteps, he looked over to the glass doors. Mr. Jefferson was coming! Mr. Jefferson pulled on one of the glass doors, and, as if by magic, both doors opened. Noting the visitor's astonished expression, he smiled as he walked into the room, explaining that the doors were connected by a chain under the floor. When one door was moved, the other door also moved.

The former president put on his glasses and read the letter of introduction. After he'd finished, he bowed and invited the visitor to dine and stay the night. Then Mr. Jefferson began to point out some interesting things in the entrance hall. Having the floor painted grass green, he told the visitor, had been suggested by Gilbert Stuart, the famous portrait painter.

Of the many items on display in the room, Mr. Jefferson was especially proud of the Native American artifacts. He

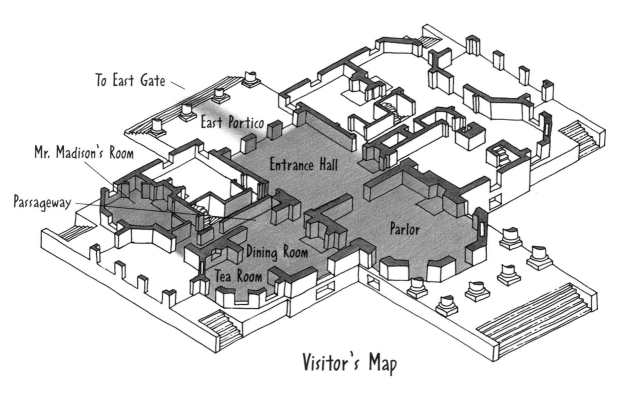

Visitor's Map

told the visitor he'd been interested in Indians ever since he was a boy. His interest led him to study their languages, and he'd begun to collect some of the things they made. He showed the visitor a cradle, a knife case, and a buffalo robe that had been painted to tell the story of a battle. The explorers Meriwether Lewis and William Clark had brought back most of the items from their famous expedition to lands to the west.

In the distance, the guest heard the sound of the dinner bell. It was five o'clock. Mr. Jefferson showed a few more of his prized possessions—the jawbone, tusk, and teeth of a mastodon—and then led the way into the dining room. In the center of the room stood a long table with many chairs around it. Servants scurried around the room, making final preparations for the meal.

In April of 1805, the explorer Meriwether Lewis sent this robe to Jefferson from what would later become North Dakota. Made of buffalo hide, the robe depicts a battle between two Native American groups, the Mandan and the Dakota.

To satisfy his desire for privacy while dining, Jefferson designed a revolving shelf unit (inset) *on which slaves could place plates without entering the room.*

Mr. Jefferson pointed out the books that lined the mantle. He liked to have books available while he waited for his family to come to dinner. No reading was required on this day, for the room was soon filled with Jefferson's family—his daughter Martha; his son-in-law, Thomas Randolph; and six of their children. This gathering was small. Usually more relatives and guests were at the table.

As the second dinner bell rang, the visitor was introduced to each of the family members. Then he stepped onto the crumb cloth that was placed on the floor to protect it from spills and took a seat at the table.

It was a wonderful meal, served from silver serving platters on beautiful porcelain plates. He drank fine wines from engraved goblets. The main dish was French-style goose, complemented by delicious applesauce. There were plenty of fresh vegetables from the garden. A new dessert called ice cream came with pastry at the end of the meal.

It was surprising to the visitor that this large meal could be served by only a few servants. Mr. Jefferson smiled and showed him to the hallway around the corner. At the end of the short hallway was a revolving door. When Mr. Jefferson pushed it open, the other side had shelves on it.

Slaves prepared the meals in a kitchen below the south terrace. They carried the cooked food along a passageway under the house then up a flight of stairs to this door. By using these shelves, only a few slaves were needed in the dining room. This gave Mr. Jefferson, his family, and friends more privacy during their meals. The visitor followed Mr. Jefferson back into the dining room and watched as he showed another interesting device, called a dumbwaiter. Built into the end of the mantle, the dumbwaiter brought wine from the cellar without another servant entering the dining area.

Later Mrs. Randolph invited the men to go into the next room for some tea. The tea room was cool, but the tea was hot, and the conversation was interesting. After a while, Mr. Jefferson suggested that they continue their

The table in the tea room is set with some of Jefferson's silver service and dishes. The view out the window is of the north terrace and pavilion.

discussion in the parlor. The visitor was happy to have the chance to see yet another room in this magnificent home. The parlor did not disappoint him. It was a large, bright room with many windows. And the floor—made of dark cherrywood squares framed with lighter beechwood—was different from anything he'd ever seen. Mr. Jefferson called it parquet and told the visitor he'd designed it to resemble floors he'd seen in France.

On the floor in front of the fireplace, a few of Mr. Jefferson's grandchildren were enjoying a board game, giggling as they took turns rolling the dice. Two other grandchildren were absorbed in a game of chess played on a

Installed in 1804, Jefferson's polished parquet floor (inset) *complemented the rest of the parlor's elegant furnishings.*

marble table. Mr. Jefferson proudly watched the game, taking turns to whisper advice to each of the youngsters.

The adults found comfortable chairs in which to sit and continue their conversation. After the children had finished their games, Mr. Jefferson asked them to entertain the group with some music. Ellen and Cornelia gladly agreed. They took turns on the harpsichord, and both played very well.

Soon after the clock struck nine, Mr. Jefferson stood and said goodnight. A slave led the visitor through the dining room, down the hall past the revolving door, and into the guest room. A fire crackled in the fireplace, bringing warmth on this cool, late spring night.

The guest room was called Mr. Madison's Room because Mr. Jefferson's friends James Madison and his wife Dolley used it on their frequent visits. The visitor sat on the alcove bed and looked around this room with eight sides. It had interesting French wallpaper of vines growing on trellises. The furniture was simple—a stand, two chairs, two mirrors, a table, and a candlestick—but the windows were not. They went all the way to the floor and could be used as doors to get outside.

The visitor put his head on the pillow but couldn't sleep. He was thinking of all the things he had seen today and wondered what he would see tomorrow. The visitor knew he would never forget this visit to Monticello.

Alcove beds were another French idea that Jefferson brought to Monticello. Most of the house's bedrooms had the beds tucked into a recessed wall, rather than jutting into the center of the room. Except for the bed in Jefferson's own suite, the alcove beds enclosed the sleeper on three sides and left the rest of the room open for other uses.

"HERE WAS BURIED
THOMAS JEFFERSON
AUTHOR OF THE
DECLARATION
OF
AMERICAN INDEPENDENCE
OF THE
STATUTE OF VIRGINIA
FOR
RELIGIOUS FREEDOM
AND FATHER OF THE
UNIVERSITY OF VIRGINIA"

Jefferson designed the original stone that marked his grave and worded the epitaph. Congress paid for a replacement stone in 1883.

[For Sale] On the fifteenth of January [1827] at Monticello ... the whole of the residue of the personal property of Thomas Jefferson ...

—Richmond *Enquirer*

Afterword

Thomas Jefferson lived in and welcomed visitors to Monticello for the next 16 years. On July 4, 1826—50 years to the day after the Declaration of Independence had been signed—Jefferson died. He was buried in the family plot that lies a short distance from Mulberry Row.

The estate had already been suffering from some neglect. There was no money to make major repairs, let alone to leave to the family. At his death, Jefferson was in debt more than $100,000, and his heirs were responsible for paying his creditors. As a result, many of the remaining slaves were sold. Most of the livestock, crops, farm equipment, household furniture, and artworks also went on the auction block.

Family members stayed at Monticello until 1829, but it, too, had to be sold to help pay the debt. Even so, visitors came, taking away souvenir clippings from the

riah Phillips Levy, who bought Monticello in 1834, had more than just an architectural interest in the famous home of Thomas Jefferson. The first Jewish commissioned officer in any branch of the U.S. military, Levy admired Jefferson's views on religious freedom. Levy believed these writings had enabled him to advance in the U.S. Navy. Uriah's nephew, Jefferson Monroe Levy, shared this appreciation and strived to keep Monticello from ruin, funding many of the repairs out of his own pocket.

garden and later chipping bits of stone from Jefferson's tomb marker. The first buyer, James Barclay, took possession in 1831 but sold the house and several hundred acres in 1834 to Uriah P. Levy, an officer in the U.S. Navy. For the next 90 years, Levy and his descendants held the property—except for a short period during the Civil War (1861–1865), when the Confederate government confiscated it. The Levys tried hard to preserve the home of the former president. They made repairs to the buildings and purchased some of the original land around the estate. Levy family members, mainly Jefferson Monroe Levy, sought out Jeffersonian heirlooms scattered throughout the country and brought them back to Monticello. Meanwhile, though, the family also changed the look of the place to suit their own tastes and those of the time.

But many Americans wanted to put Monticello under public ownership. Finally, in 1923, the Thomas Jefferson Memorial Foundation was created. The foundation bought

Jefferson's carefully documented records of his gardens have enabled restorers to faithfully recreate the groves, orchards, and flower beds.

Visitors make the trek up the mountain to see Jefferson's home and to experience a little of how it was at Monticello.

Monticello from Jefferson Monroe Levy and began the long process of repairing and restoring it. Armed with research, workers replaced furnishings, made structural repairs, and restored the gardens. By the 1950s, after even more renovations, Monticello and its surroundings looked much as they had in Jefferson's time. A later archaeological effort explained the placement of original garden walls, planting patterns, and buildings along Mulberry Row.

In 1993, to celebrate Jefferson's 250th birthday, the foundation mounted an exhibition that brought together many more original Jeffersonian treasures. Every year the house and grounds welcome more than 500,000 people to this famous American landmark.

Glossary

Doric order: A simple, classical design for a column that follows styles common in ancient Greece. Throughout Monticello, Jefferson used classical styles, which he studied in the writings of the Italian architect Andrea Palladio (1508–1580).

pavilion: A small, ornamental building that sits at the end of a terrace.

piazza: A long, open space usually with a roof supported by columns.

plantation: A large estate on which crops are grown by workers who live on the estate. In Jefferson's time, plantation owners usually used slave labor.

portico: A roofed space that forms the entrance to the front of a large house.

terrace: A level walkway in front of a building. In Monticello's case, the terraces extended away from the north and south ends of the house.

Pronunciation Guide

fruitery	FROOD-uh-ree
Monticello	mahn-tuh-CHEH-loh
pavilion	puh-VIHL-yuhn
piazza	pee-AH-zuh
privy	PRIH-vee

Further Reading

Bruns, Roger. *Thomas Jefferson.* New York: Chelsea House, 1986.

Ferris, Jeri Chase. *Thomas Jefferson: Father of Liberty.* Minneapolis: Carolrhoda Books, Inc., 1998.

Fisher, Leonard Everett. *Monticello.* New York: Holiday House, 1988.

Meltzer, Milton. *Thomas Jefferson: The Revolutionary Aristocrat.* New York: Franklin Watts, 1991.

Morris, Jeffrey. *The Jefferson Way.* Minneapolis: Lerner Publications Company, 1994.

Ofosu-Appiah, L. H. *People in Bondage.* Minneapolis: Runestone Press, 1995.

Reef, Catherine. *Monticello.* New York: Dillon Press, 1991.

Sirvaitis, Karen. *Virginia.* Minneapolis: Lerner Publications Company, 1991.

Touring Information

Monticello is open every day of the year, except Christmas Day. Hours are 8:00 A.M. to 5:00 P.M., March to November, and 9:00 A.M. to 4:30 P.M., November to March. The estate is located on State Route 53 at Monticello Mountain. For more information about visiting Monticello,

write to:
Business and Public Affairs
Post Office Box 316
Charlottesville, Virginia 22902

or call:
(804) 984-9822

Index

About the Author

Robert Young, a prolific author of children's books, created the series *How It Was* to enable readers to tour famous landmarks through the experiences of the people who did or may have lived, worked, or visited there. Robert, who makes his home in Eugene, Oregon, teaches elementary school, as well as visits schools around the country to talk with students about writing and curiosity. Among Robert's other literary credits are *Money* and *Game Day*, titles published by Carolrhoda Books, Inc.

Acknowledgments

For quoted material: p. 5, Anthony M. Brescia, ed., *The Letters and Papers of Richard Rush* (Wilmington, DE: Microfilm edition, 1980); p. 6, B. L. Rayner, *Life of Thomas Jefferson* (Boston: Lilly, Wait, Colman, & Holden, 1834); p. 11, Natalie S. Bober, *Thomas Jefferson: Man on a Mountain* (New York: Aladdin Paperbacks, 1997); p. 21, Rayford W. Logan, ed., *Memoirs of a Monticello Slave* (Charlottesville: University of Virginia Press, 1951); p. 27, Logan, *Memoirs;* p. 31, Sarah N. Randolph, *The Domestic Life of Thomas Jefferson.* Reprint (Charlottesville: University Press of Virginia, 1985); p. 41, Merrill D. Peterson, ed., *Visitors to Monticello* (Charlottesville: University Press of Virginia, 1989); p. 47, Randolph, *Domestic Life;* p. 57, Announcement in the Richmond *Enquirer*, January 9, 1827.
For photos and artwork: © Paul Rocheleau, pp. 4, 16, 18, 32 (left), 46, 51; © Monticello/Thomas Jefferson Memorial Foundation, pp. 6, 17 (top), 23, 31, 32 (right), 34, 36, 45, 51 (inset), 54 (inset); © Eugene G. Schulz, pp. 7, 9, 17 (bottom), 56, 60; © Robert Lautman, pp. 10, 35, 40; © Langdon Clay, pp. 13, 14, 15, 30, 37, 38, 39, 44, 48, 53, 55; © Kenneth Garrett, p. 19; MPLIC, p. 22; State Dept. of Archives and History, Raleigh, NC, p. 24; © R. Perron, pp. 25, 59; Mss. Print Coll., Special Coll. Dept., Univ. of VA Lib., p. 27; Lib. of Congress, p. 28; Peabody Museum–Harvard University/Photo by Hillel Burger, p. 50; Charlottesville/Albemarle Convention and Visitors Bureau, p. 54; U.S. Naval Academy Museum, p. 58. All maps and artwork, except for pp. 5, 11, and 31, by Bryan Liedahl. Cover: © Paul Rocheleau. Title page: © Monticello/Thomas Jefferson Memorial Foundation.